Editor   Karen Barker
Language Consultant   Betty Root
Natural History Consultant   Dr Gerald Legg

Carolyn Scrace is a graduate of Brighton
College of Art in England, specializing in design
and illustration. She has worked in animation,
advertising and children's fiction and non-fiction.
She is a major contributor to the popular
Worldwise series and *The X-ray Picture Book*
series, particularly **Amazing Animals**, **Your Body**,
and **Dinosaurs**.

Betty Root was the Director of the Reading
and Language Information Center at the University
of Reading in England for over twenty years. She
has worked on numerous children's books, both
fiction and non-fiction.

Dr Gerald Legg holds a doctorate in zoology
from Manchester University in England. His current
position is biologist at the Booth Museum of Natural
History in Brighton, England.

David Salariya was born in Dundee, Scotland,
where he studied illustration and printmaking,
concentrating on book design in his post graduate
year. He has designed and created many new series
of children's books.

An SBC Book conceived, edited and designed by
The Salariya Book Company
25 Marlborough Place, Brighton BN1 1UB

First published in Great Britain in 1999 by Franklin Watts

First American edition 2000 by Franklin Watts/Children's Press
A Division of Scholastic Inc.
557 Broadway,
New York, NY 10012

Printed in China, Shenzhen
March 2015
PO 453398

Library of Congress Cataloging-in-Publication Data

Scrace, Carolyn.
    The journey of a butterfly / written and illustrated by
Carolyn Scrace; created & designed by David Salariya.
        p.   cm. --- (Lifecycles)
    Includes index.
    Summary: Describes the life cycle and annual migration
of the monarch butterfly.
    ISBN 0-531-14518-2 (lib. bdg)
    ISBN 0-531-15417-3 (pbk)
    1. Monarch butterfly--Migration--Juvenile literature.
[1. Monarch Butterfly. 2. Butterflies.] I. Salariya, David.
II. Title. III. Series.
QL561.D3S27 1999   98-28652
                                                          CIP

AC

lifecycles

The Journey of a Butterfly

Written and Illustrated by Carolyn Scrace

Created and Designed by David Salariya

W

Franklin Watts®

A Division of Scholastic Inc.
New York Toronto London Auckland Sydney
Mexico City New Delhi Hong Kong
Danbury, Connecticut

Butterflies are insects with long bodies
and large, brightly colored wings.
In the fall, monarch butterflies fly
from the cold north to the warm south
of North America (see map, page 26).
There they spend the winter
half asleep in the trees. In the spring,
they fly back north.

Their journey is called a *migration*.
In this book you can follow the
amazing migration of
the monarch butterfly.

During the summer, monarch butterflies live in Canada and the northern United States.

They spend all summer feeding.

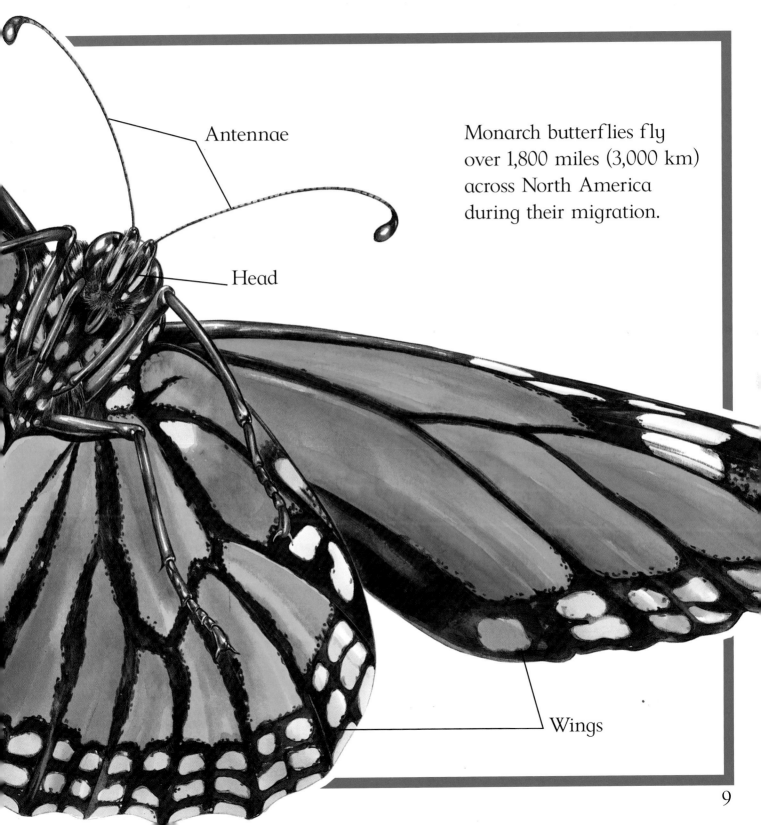

Antennae

Head

Wings

Monarch butterflies fly over 1,800 miles (3,000 km) across North America during their migration.

9

In the fall it gets cold. There is less food for butterflies to eat.

The butterflies gather in groups to start the long migration south to California and Mexico.

The wings of a monarch butterfly are big and strong. They help it to fly quickly and for long distances.

The groups get larger as more and more butterflies join them.

At night, thousands of butterflies land on trees to rest.

Each morning
they continue
flying south.

13

In early winter
the butterflies reach
the warm south.
In their thousands,
they settle on the trunks
and branches of certain trees.
All through the winter
the butterflies stay there, half asleep.
This is called semihibernation.

The butterflies
use the same trees
every year.

15

In the spring,
the butterflies wake up.
They are ready
to start the long flight
back north.

For this return
journey, the
butterflies fly
on their own and
not in large groups.

During the journey north, male and female butterflies mate. The females stop to lay their eggs along the way. Then the adult butterflies die.

The tiny eggs from the female butterfly stick to the leaves where they are laid.

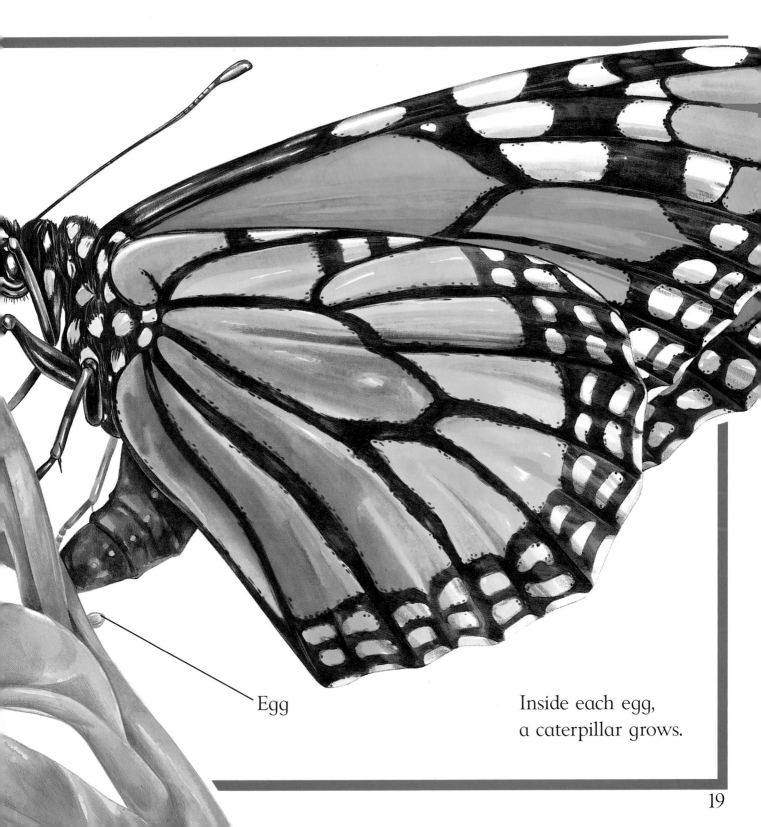

Egg

Inside each egg,
a caterpillar grows.

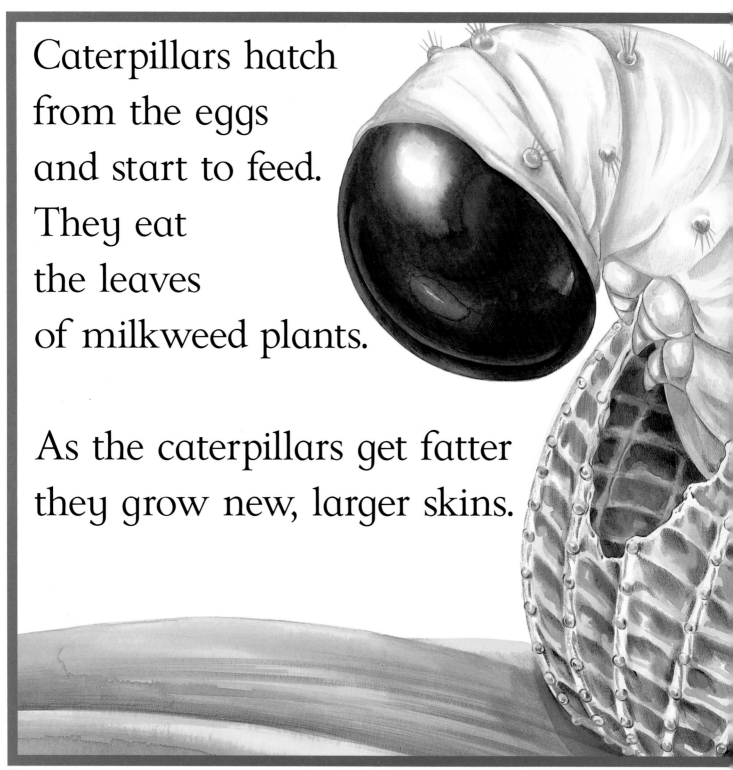

Caterpillars hatch
from the eggs
and start to feed.
They eat
the leaves
of milkweed plants.

As the caterpillars get fatter
they grow new, larger skins.

Milkweed is poisonous
to other animals.
Eating milkweed
makes the caterpillars
poisonous too.
This means
other animals
do not eat them.

21

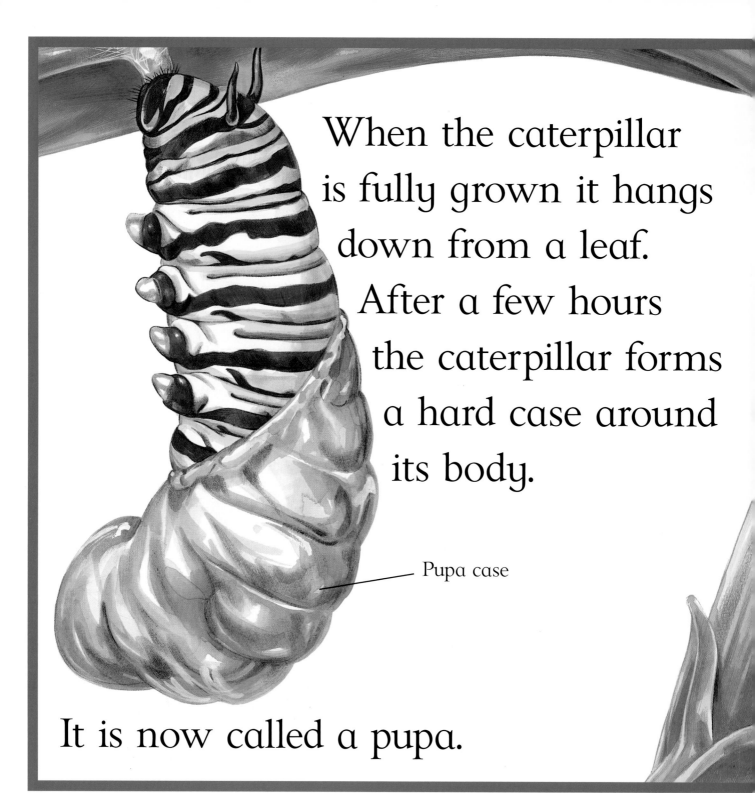

When the caterpillar
is fully grown it hangs
down from a leaf.
After a few hours
the caterpillar forms
a hard case around
its body.

Pupa case

It is now called a pupa.

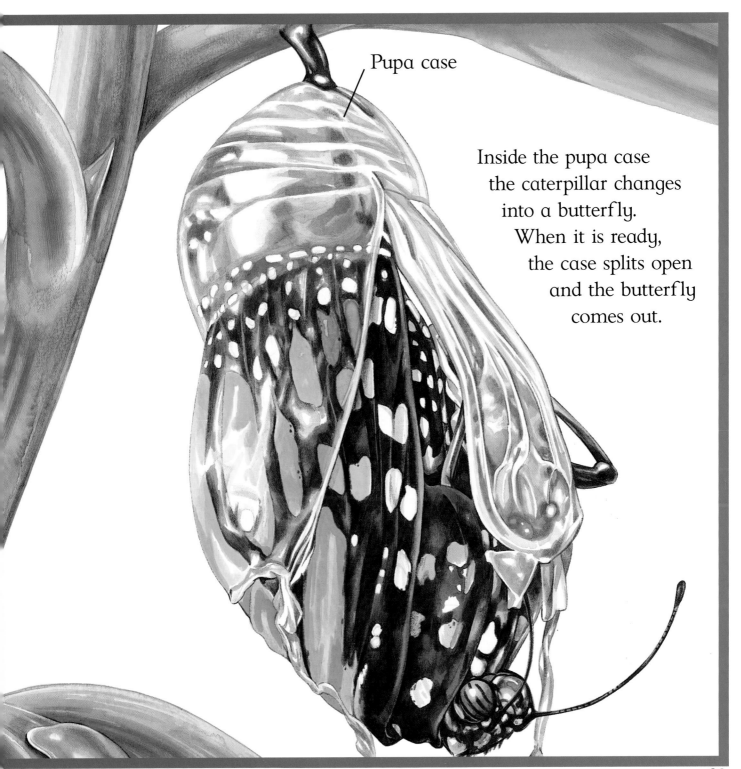

Pupa case

Inside the pupa case
the caterpillar changes
into a butterfly.
When it is ready,
the case splits open
and the butterfly
comes out.

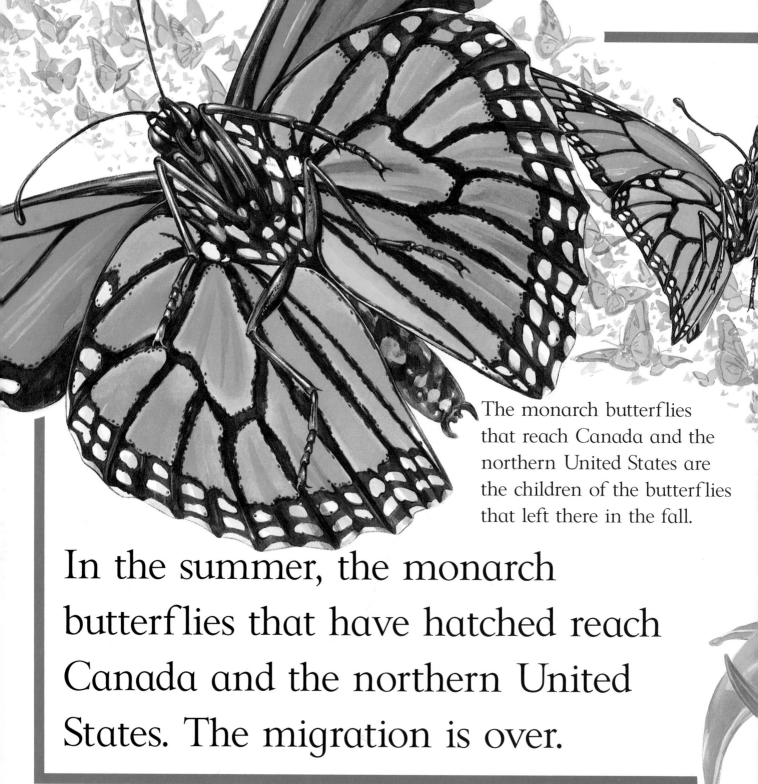

The monarch butterflies that reach Canada and the northern United States are the children of the butterflies that left there in the fall.

In the summer, the monarch butterflies that have hatched reach Canada and the northern United States. The migration is over.

The butterflies live in the north all summer. In the fall, it will be their turn to fly south. The migration will start once again.

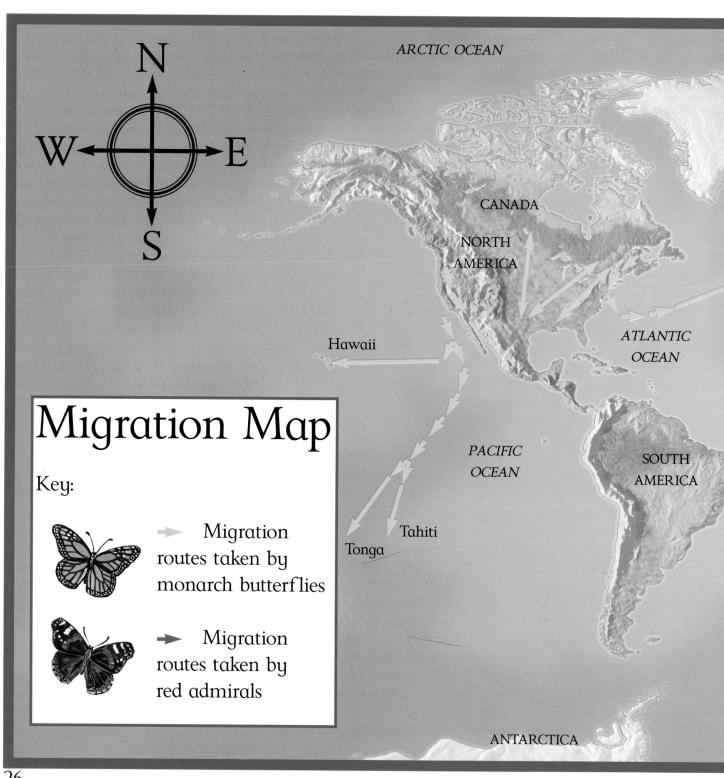

N
W E
S

ARCTIC OCEAN

CANADA

NORTH
AMERICA

Hawaii

ATLANTIC
OCEAN

Migration Map

Key:

PACIFIC
OCEAN

SOUTH
AMERICA

Migration
routes taken by
monarch butterflies

Tahiti

Tonga

Migration
routes taken by
red admirals

ANTARCTICA

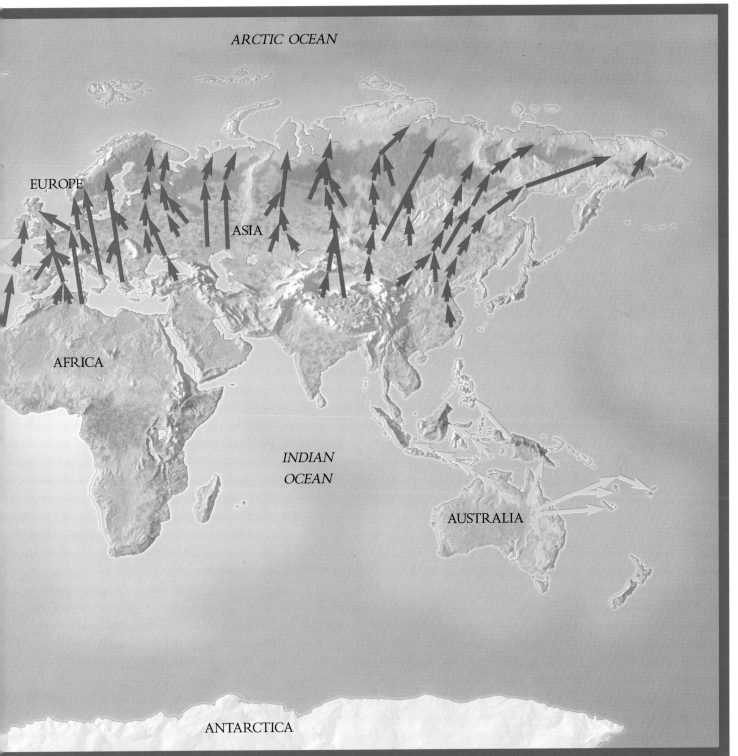

ARCTIC OCEAN

EUROPE

ASIA

AFRICA

INDIAN

OCEAN

AUSTRALIA

ANTARCTICA

27

Butterfly Words

Antennae
The feelers on the head of an insect

Caterpillar
The stage in the life of a butterfly between hatching from an egg and forming a pupa

Flight
A journey made by flying through the air

Hatch
When the caterpillar comes out of its egg

Insect
An animal with six legs and two antennae. The body of an insect is divided into three parts and is covered with a hard skin

Mating
When a male and female join together to make a baby

Poisonous
When something produces a substance that can kill or sicken the animal that eats it

Pupa
The stage in the life of a butterfly between being a caterpillar and becoming an adult butterfly

Semihibernation
When an animal is half asleep all through winter

Index